in the

ci**t**y

i-SPY

INTRODUCTION

Cities are busy places, full of hustle and bustle, with plenty to see and do. Whether you are looking for cafés and restaurants, shops and markets, or museums and attractions, cities are great places to visit or to live in.

Historically, cities were set up for trade and for this reason many of them are built on rivers, which allowed ships to come in and bring goods from overseas. Nowadays, cities are still important internationally although methods of transportation and communication have changed. Cities are bases for governments, organisations and universities, and often have interesting histories full of significant people and events.

Typically, cities have high population densities, which means lots of people live in a relatively small area. When you go to a city, you will notice that the roads and streets are busy and that there are lots of amenities to cater to everyone's needs, as well as many events and activities to keep people entertained.

As you take in the many sights, sounds and smells in the city, use your i-SPY book to keep a record of all the exciting things you come across, collecting points along the way!

How to use your i-SPY book

As you work through this book, you will notice that the entries are arranged in groups based on what type of entry they are and where you might find them. You need 1000 points to send off for your i-SPY certificate (see page 64) but that is not too difficult because there are masses of points in every book. Each entry has a star or circle and points value beside it. The stars represent harder to spot entries. As you make each i-SPY, write your score in the circle or star.

Points: 5

BUS STOP

They come in all shapes and sizes. Some are open, some offer shelter. Score for any.

BIKE PARK

Points: 10

If you are using your bike, you may want to park it while you do something else in the city centre.

PHONE BOX

Points: 25

There used to be many phone boxes in the streets but now there are fewer because lots of people have mobile phones.

Points: 5

POSTBOX

Mail deposited in post boxes is collected and sorted at a delivery office, then it is sent out with a post man or woman to be delivered to people's houses.

LITTER BIN

Points: 5

Most city centre footpaths are well served with bins. They help keep the streets clear of rubbish and save you from having to take your litter home.

COLOURED BIN

Points: 10

Sometimes cities have bigger coloured bins that can take the rubbish from several flats or small businesses in one go.

Points: 15

RECYCLING BINS

Recycling bins accept different materials such as cardboard, aluminium and plastic, that can be processed and used again.

5 **Points: 5**

LITTER

Litter which has been dropped or blown out of bins looks untidy and can encourage pests

PIGEONS EATING DISCARDED FOOD

Points: 15 **15**

Pigeons peck at discarded food they find. Not everyone likes them – they're often considered a nuisance.

GUTTER

Points: 5

5

Gutters direct rainwater to drains to avoid build ups which might cause flooding or damage.

5

Points: 5

DRAIN

Water filters down drains into sewers.

MANHOLE

Points: 10

10

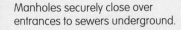

Manholes securely close over entrances to sewers underground.

Points: 10

ROADWORKS SIGN

These signs tell road users to take care as there are roadworks ahead.

CLOSED ROAD

Points: 20

For major roadworks the whole road needs to be closed and traffic has to be temporarily directed along other routes.

Points: 5

ROAD CONE

Traffic or road cones are often used across the country to mark off parts of the steet that are closed or being repaired.

9

PERSON DIRECTING TRAFFIC

Points: 25

Traffic co-ordinators point directions with their hands or start and stop traffic by using signs on posts.

ROAD DRILL

Noisy pneumatic drills dig up the road so repairs can be done.

CEMENT MIXER

Points: 25

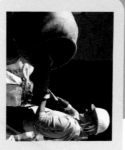

The barrel of a cement mixer spins around, combining the sand and water to make cement.

STEAMROLLER

Points: 20

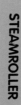

Steamrollers can be seen at the site of road works smoothing down newly applied road surfaces such as tarmac.

11

MARKINGS BEING PAINTED

Top Spot! Points: 50

Street lines have to be repainted after road repairs or once they've worn off over time. Have you ever noticed that road markings are long and thin? This is so that drivers can read them as they are moving along the road.

LOADING BAY

Whether a sign
or road marking,
loading bays
show delivery
drivers where
to park for easy
access to a
building.

PARENT AND CHILD PARKING BAY

Points: 10

Look for wider
parking spaces
for people with
young children
to use.

Points: 10

Bulky objects and parcels are moved around in delivery vans.

Points: 20

Couriers travel the city on foot, on bicycles, and in vans to deliver post. To collect these 20 points, try to find one on a bike.

Points: 15

Post office employees collect and deliver post each day, by vehicle and on foot.

Points: 15

Food orders such as pizza are delivered quickly to the customer whilst still hot.

Points: 10

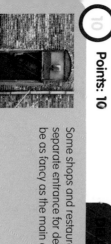

Some shops and resturants have a separate entrance for deliveries. It may not be as fancy as the main entrance!

BIN LORRY

Points: 15

Bin lorries travel around collecting rubbish from bins. Each neighbourhood has its own bin collection day, and this may differ depending on which type of rubbish is being picked up.

REFUSE COLLECTOR

Points: 15

Refuse collectors hop on and off bin lorries collecting rubbish bins to tip into the back.

Points: 25

STREET CLEANER

People with brushes and hand operated litter picker sticks pick up scraps of rubbish on the street.

STREET SWEEPER VEHICLE

Points: 20

Street sweepers slowly drive around sweeping up litter with their brushes.

SKIP

Points: 15 15

Skips are large temporary bins for industrial refuse. Once used, they're emptied at landfill sites.

Points: 50   Top Spot!

RECYCLING PLANT

Visiting a recycling plant can be very interesting. Different kinds of materials such as plastic can be processed and reused.

Points: 5

LEAFLETS

Leaflets are a way to share information about a local business, a tourist attraction, or an upcoming event.

CONCERT POSTER

BOX OFFICE

Points: 15

Performers on tour can visit many cities. Posters advertising shows or events include important information such as the venue, date and time. They may also have big pictures to grab your attention.

Points: 10

Start today

BILLBOARD

Billboards have been in use for centuries and could be hand-painted in the past.

19

VIDEO BOARD

Modern electronic billboards are eye-catching and can cycle through more than one advertisement.

Points: 10

FREESHEET NEWSPAPER/ MAGAZINE

Free newspapers and magazines can be found at busy places like train stations. They make money through advertising inside.

CHARITY COLLECTOR

Points: 20

On a busy street you might see some people collecting change for charities. Sometimes they are paid by the charities involved, but often the collectors will be volunteers who give their time for free.

NEON SIGN

Points: 5

Bright neon signs bring the city to life at night-time.

FREE TASTERS

Points: 20

Free tasters offered in some shops let customers sample food before they buy.

10

Points: 10

SKYSCRAPER

kyscrapers are often the first thing we see when approaching a city.
e tallest building in the United Kingdom is the Shard in London.

FIRE ESCAPE

Points: 15

Fire escapes are attached to the side of tall buildings to provide an additional exit route.

 **Points: 25**

GARGOYLE

Look up! Gargoyles were originally designed as gutter-ends. Now they are mostly decorative.

(10) **Points: 10**

BRIDGE

Bridges can be very old and have historic significance. They are also constructed in lots of different ways. See how many types you can spot.

CHINATOWN ARCH

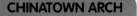

Top Spot!   **Points: 40**

These decorative arches are positioned at the entrance to 'Chinatowns', areas with a lot of Chinese businesses and restaurants.

Points: 25

FOUNTAIN

This fountain is in Cardiff, but there are many to be found in cities around the world. The Jet d'Eau in Lake Geneva shoots water 140 metres high.

Points: 10

Scaffolding is a series of temporary platforms that allow workers access to the outside of a building to finish construction or carry out repairs.

REFUSE CHUTE

Points: 20

To save time, building site rubbish can be sent down refuse chutes directly into a skip.

27

HARD HATS

Points: 10 (10)

Building sites can be dangerous places. Hard hats offer protection from falling objects.

(5) **Points: 5**

HI-VIS

Hi-visibility clothing is brightly coloured so the wearer can be seen from a distance, preventing accidents.

(5) **Points: 5**

RETAIL PARK

Retail parks are often on the edges of cities and offer more room to accommodate big shops.

SHOPPING MALL

Points: 5 (5)

Handy when it's raining, indoor shopping malls have a roof overhead.

COFFEE SHOP

Points: 5

The first coffee shop in the UK was opened in Oxford in 1652. Today, they are one of the most common shops on the high street. They usually offer a wide range of sandwiches and baked goods alongside tea, coffee and cold drinks.

Points: 10

POST OFFICE

Post offices offer services such as passport and driving license forms as well as handling post.

Points: 10

BAKERY

Bakers start their working day very early to bake fresh bread for morning customers.

PET SHOP

Points: 15

Some pet shops offer free biscuits and water to dogs visiting with their owners.

TOYSHOP

Points: 15

Perhaps you found this i-SPY book in a toyshop!

Points: 15 15

BUTCHER

Alongside beef and pork, some butchers offer more unusual meats such as kangaroo.

Points: 20

 FISHMONGER

Fishmongers keep fish fresh by storing and displaying it on ice cold trays.

FLORIST

Points: 20

Florists get their flower supply from early morning markets.

Points: 20

THEATRE

Bonus five points for spotting a tucked-away stage door entrance where actors come and go.

LIBRARY

Points: 15 15

Libraries are places where historically you went to read or borrow books. These days most libraries offer a range of facilities such as online access terminals and cafés.

25 **Points: 25**

SWIMMING POOL

Outdoor swimming pools are called lidos.

Points: 25

ICE RINK

When the rink is closed, special vehicles glide over the ice to keep it smooth and clean.

Points: 40   Top Spot!

SNOW SLOPE

Modern technology can create snow slopes indoors by controlling the climate.

FOOD MARKET

Points: 20

Some market sellers call out to passing customers to attract them to their stall.

Points: 20

HOT DOG STAND

Hot dog stands are usually temporary structures which can be taken away at the end of the day.

15 **Points: 15**

NEWSPAPER STAND

Sometimes newspapers and magazines in other languages are available at newspaper stands too.

MUSEUM

Points: 15 15

Muesums come in all shapes and sizes. At many newer museums even the buildings themselves are works of art.

MOBILE PHONE SHOP

Points: 10

Sometimes phones break! Mobile phone shops often offer repair services as well as selling products.

Points: 10

CHARITY SHOP

These shops are a way for charities to make money for good causes by selling second-hand items donated by the public.

ZOO

Points: 25

Zoos offer the opportunity to see animals from all over the world in one place.

Points: 10

DEPOSIT BOX

Some banks have deposit boxes where customers can post correspondence outside of opening hours.

CASH MACHINE

Points: 5

Cash machines allow people to take money from their bank accounts by entering a bank card and PIN number.

Points: 15

SELF-STORAGE

Sometimes space is tight in cities. Storage companies offer the rental of space for a fee.

WIFI

Points: 5

Wifi symbols show there is an internet signal in the area. Often the shop or café owner may charge for wifi, but sometimes it is free.

Points: 10

TOURIST INFORMATION STATION

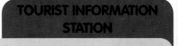

These stations help visitors looking for directions, recommendations, or travel information.

Points: 5

SANDWICH BOARD

Some chalk sandwich boards are illustrated or have funny slogans written on them.

BABY CHANGING

Points: 5

Parents travelling with small children can use specially equipped cubicles to change nappies.

Points: 5

NO SMOKING

Smoking has been banned in many public places to limit health dangers from second-hand smoke.

PARK AND RIDE SCHEME

Points: 20

Park and Ride schemes let people park their car a long way from the city centre and then travel in on a bus, train or tram. They help keep pollution and congestion levels down in the busiest areas.

Points: 15

CHARGING STATION

Electric cars are environmentally friendly and are becoming increasingly popular. Now that there are more on the roads, you might be able to spot places where they can be charged up.

Points: 15

LOST PROPERTY

In busy cities items will often be dropped or forgotten. Objects that have been accidentally left behind, can be claimed by their owners at a later date from a Lost Property station.

FIRST AID OR LIFESAVING EQUIPMENT

Points: 10

First Aid stations help people who have fallen ill or been injured, while lifesaving equipment may be found beside areas of open water and other city hazards.

Points: 20

CLOAKROOM

Sometimes, for a fee, a cloakroom will store luggage or jackets while visitors browse a museum or gallery.

STREET ART

There are all kinds of street art dotted about our cities, from paintings and statues to painted statues!

Points: 25

Colourful murals can be purely decorative, or depict an area's history.

GRAFFITI

Points: 15

Sometimes graffiti can cover entire trains, but writing on a surface without permission is illegal.

STREET MAGICIAN

Points: 25

Street magicians are used to practising their performance in front of the public.

Points: 15

BUSKER OR STREET MUSICIAN

Some people play instruments on the street, often to attract change from passers by. This one is playing the bagpipes but score points for any street musician.

FESTIVAL

Festivals are lively events, usually involving musical and theatrical performances and parades. There are sometimes even firework displays in the evenings! The Edinburgh Festival Fringe is one of the most popular of these and has been running since 1947.

OUTDOOR FILM SCREENING

Top Spot!

Points: 40

These special events project a film onto a big screen in a public place, such as a city square or park.

PROTEST

Points: 20

Protesters march or hold placards to show that they disagree with something, such as a law.

Points: 25

MASCOT

Cuddly mascots bring characters to life. Get your photograph taken with one for an extra ten points.

BALLOON FLOATED AWAY

Points: 15

Balloons which have floated away can sometimes be seen in the ceilings of stations and shops, or they may escape into the sky.

CCTV

Points: 5 (5)

CCTV stands for 'Closed Circuit Television' and monitors public places with video cameras that record what is going on.

(10) **Points: 10**

PUBLIC INFORMATION LOUDSPEAKER

Messages to travellers are played to announce platforms or share security information.

SECURITY GUARD

Points: 5 (5)

Security guards can monitor CCTV footage as well as keep a look out in person.

Points: 25

**CARDBOARD CUT-OUT
SECURITY GUARD**

Cardboard cut-outs can act as a deterrent by giving the impression a guard is watching.

PIGEON

Points: 5

There are lots of pigeons in cities. Sometimes they perch on statues.

Points: 5

SEAGULL

Despite the 'sea' in their name, many seagulls have made a home in cities. City birds can become quite used to people so watch out for one coming to steal your lunch!

15 **Points: 15**

SPARROW

Sparrows and other small birds hop around looking for crumbs.

MAGPIE

Points: 5 **5**

Magpies are common birds with distinctive black and white plumage. They also like to collect shiny objects!

FOX

Points: 15

Foxes are much more common in cities than in the countryside these days. They are nocturnal animals, so keep a lookout to spot one at night!

 **Points: 10**

SQUIRREL

Squirrels can be seen in parks or urban areas where food can be found.

54

Points: 25

DEER

Deer can sometimes be found in parks and green spaces within cities.

HEDGEHOG

 Top Spot! Points: 35

If you are very lucky you might spot one on a city street at night!

GUIDE DOG

Points: 20

Guide dogs assist blind and visually impaired people to navigate the city.

Points: 50 **Top Spot!**

SNIFFER DOG

These hard working dogs are trained to help the authorities search for illegal substances.

Points: 25

POLICE HORSE

Mounted police are sometimes used in cities when there are very large crowds like outside major sporting events or when there is a street protest. The police on horseback are able to see above the heads of the crowd and can move quickly if they need to attend an incident.

ROOFTOP GARDEN

Points: 20

If you look up you might see greenery at the top of a building.

Points: 5

HANGING BASKET

Many city walls are decorated with colourful hanging baskets.

10 Points: 10

WINDOW BOXES

Window boxes attached to windows are a way to plant flowers without a garden.

FLOWERPOTS

Points: 5 **5**

You will see all kinds of flowerpots dotted around the city. On the main streets they may have been planted by the local council to brighten up the city, but most are placed by residents outside their homes.

FUN FLOWERPOT OR DISPLAY

Points: 25

All kinds of items can be used to make unusual flowerpots or more interesting displays. Score for spotting any flower planted in something that makes you smile!

Points: 5 ⑤

BENCH

On city streets or more commonly in city parks, benches offer a welcome rest or somewhere to stop and enjoy lunch.

WEEDS

Points: 5 ⑤

Even on concrete, weeds can grow up through cracks.

PARK

Points: 5 5

Parks are usually calmer places and allow us to experience nature in the middle of the city.

INDEX

i-SPY

How to get your i-SPY certificate and badge

Let us know when you've become a super-spotter with 1000 points and we'll send you a special certificate and badge!

HERE'S WHAT TO DO!

- Ask an adult to check your score.

- Visit www.collins.co.uk/i-SPY to apply for your certificate. If you are under the age of 13 you will need a parent or guardian to do this.

- We'll send your certificate via email and you'll receive a brilliant badge through the post!